The Photographs Have Been Taken in Szopienice

By Jacek Lidwin

Copyright Jacek Lidwin 2013

Table of Contents

Title Page 1

Table of Contents 3

Introduction 5

Pictures of People and Places 7

About the History of Upper Silesia and Szopienice 46

About the Book 46

About the Author 46

introduction

walk, go, look, see, view, observe, watch, peep, survey, seek, search, meet, talk, interview, converse, chat, ask, inquire, photograph, take picture, shot

man, woman, girl, boy, human, person, people, folks, parent, mother, father, grandmother, grandfather, wife, husband, child, couple, occupant, citizen, homeless, teacher, pupil, employee, worker, metallurgist, miner, salesman, caretaker, pensioner, unemployed, walker, stroller, dog,

photography, photo, photogram, image, picture, shot, still, portrait, black, white,

street, place, square, plant, backstreet, yard, bus-stop, church, house, building, fabric, factory, school, shop, bar, pub, window, door

kissing, hugging, playing, observation, carrying, smiling, sunbathing, mass, first communion, talking, shopping, sweep

March - May 2003, Katowice - Szopienice, Upper Silesia, Poland.

Pictures of People and Places

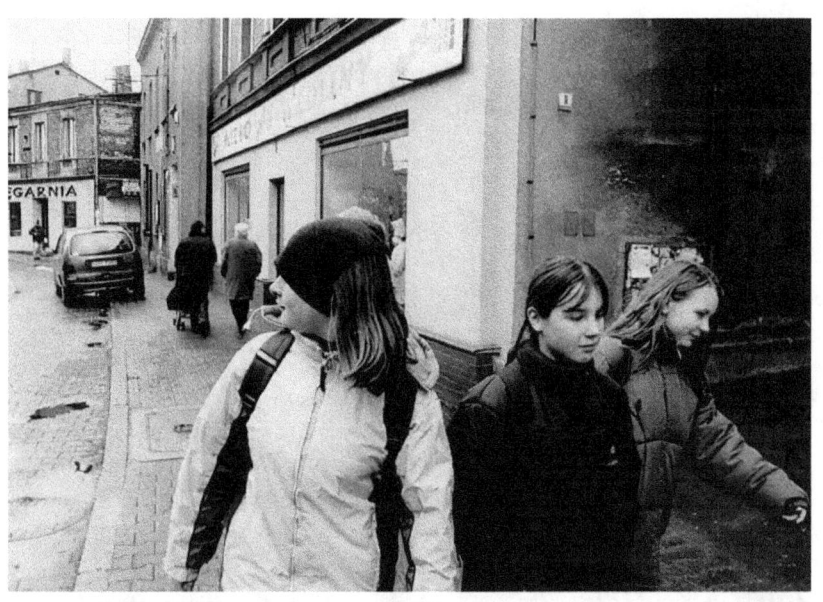

The Children run out from the school

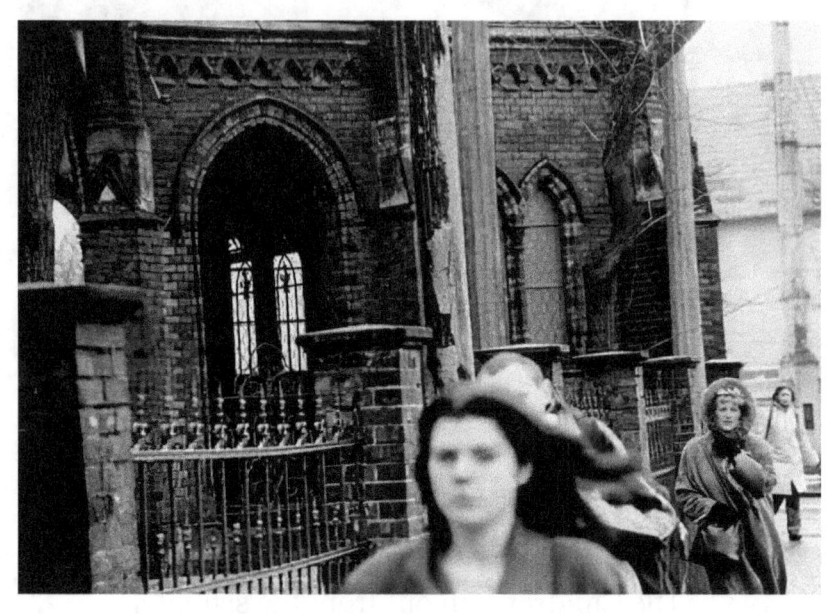

Blurry woman near church

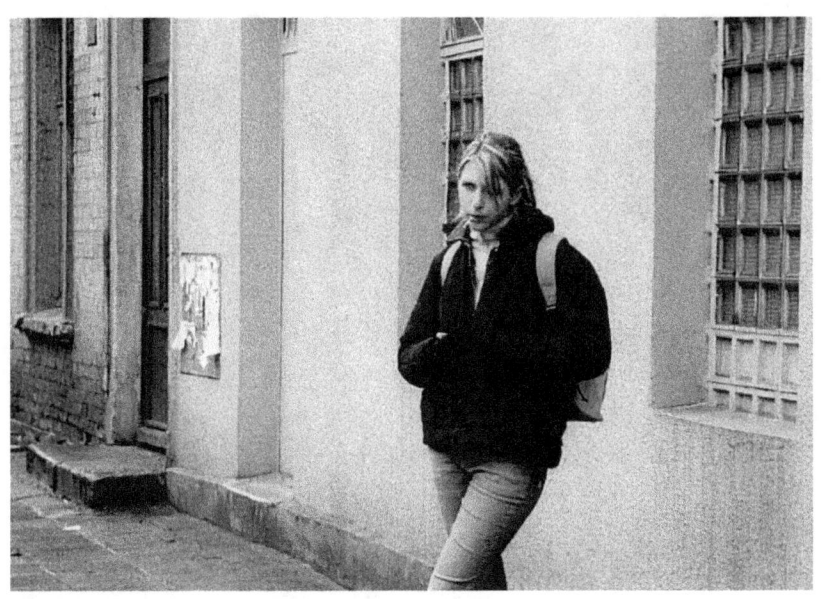

Young girl should not smoke

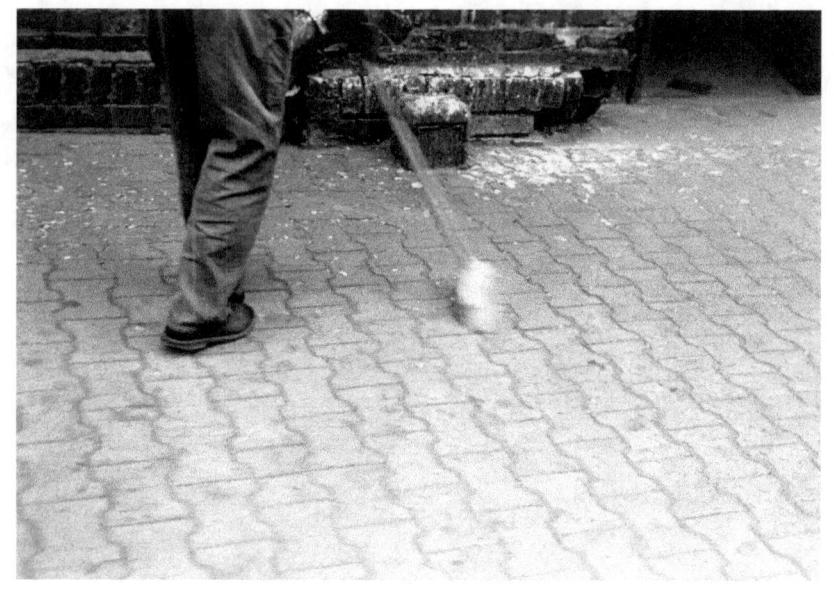

Daily sweeping is important

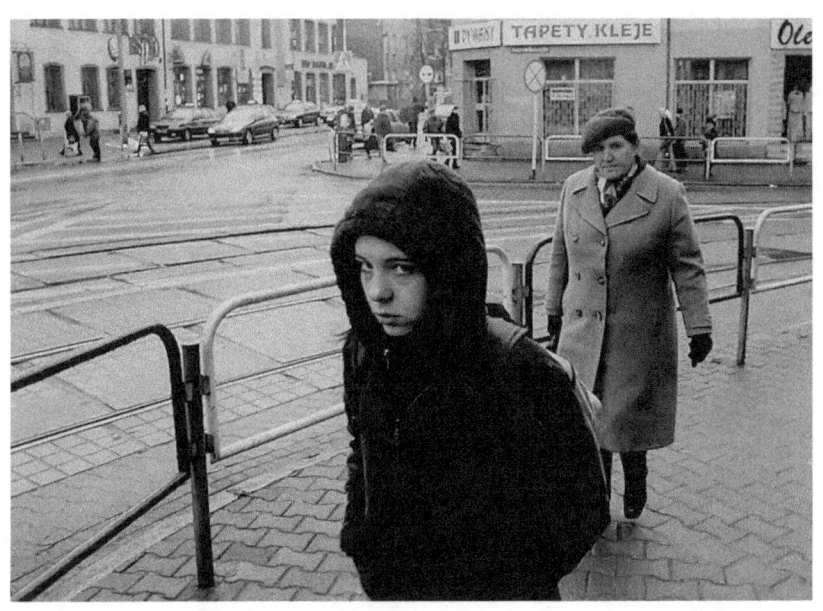

Why?

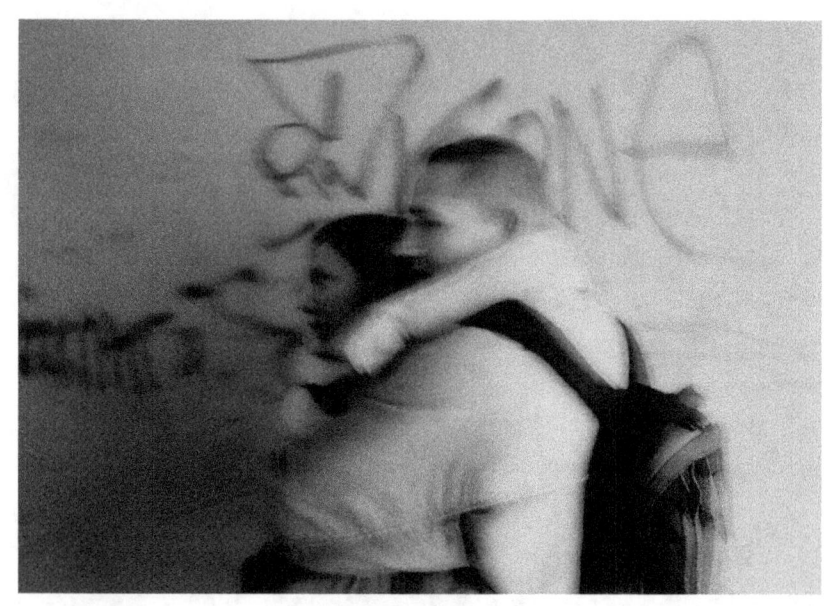

Simple affection.

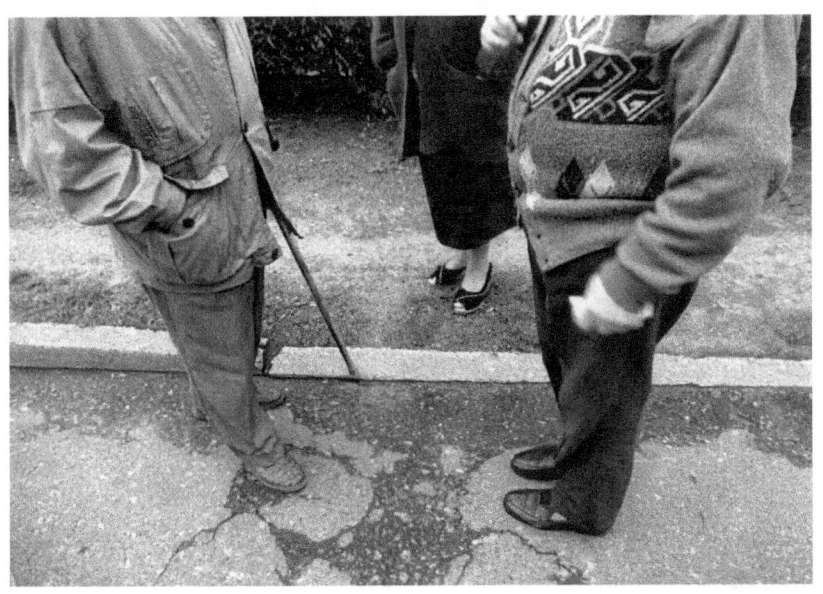

Together

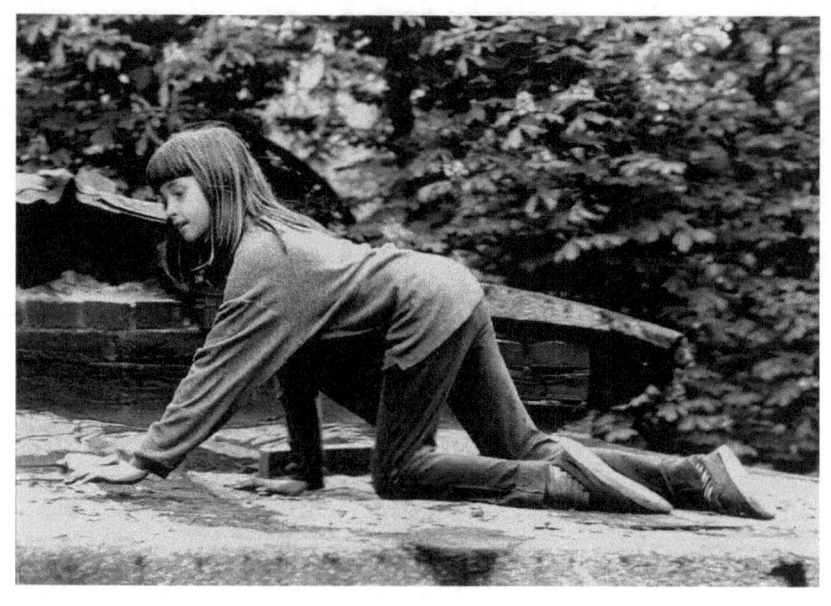

Cat on a black roof

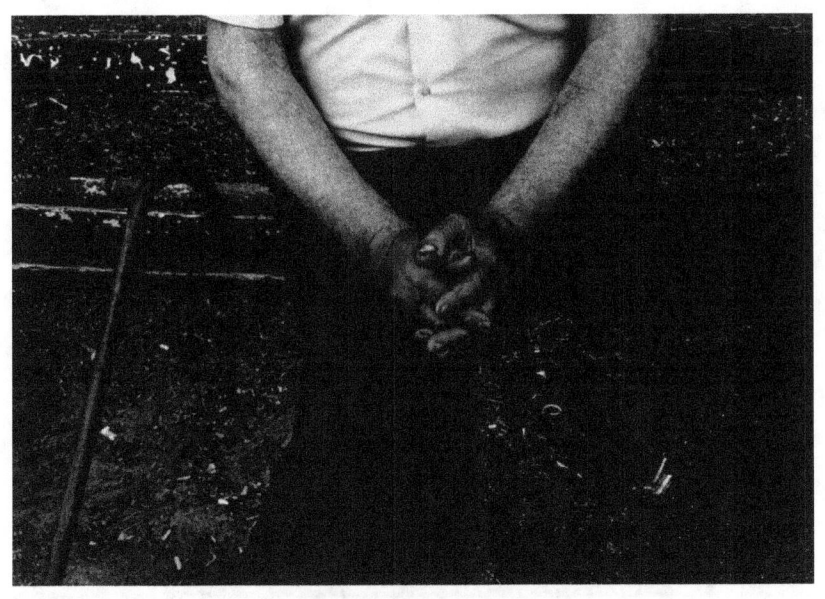

I'll tell you my story

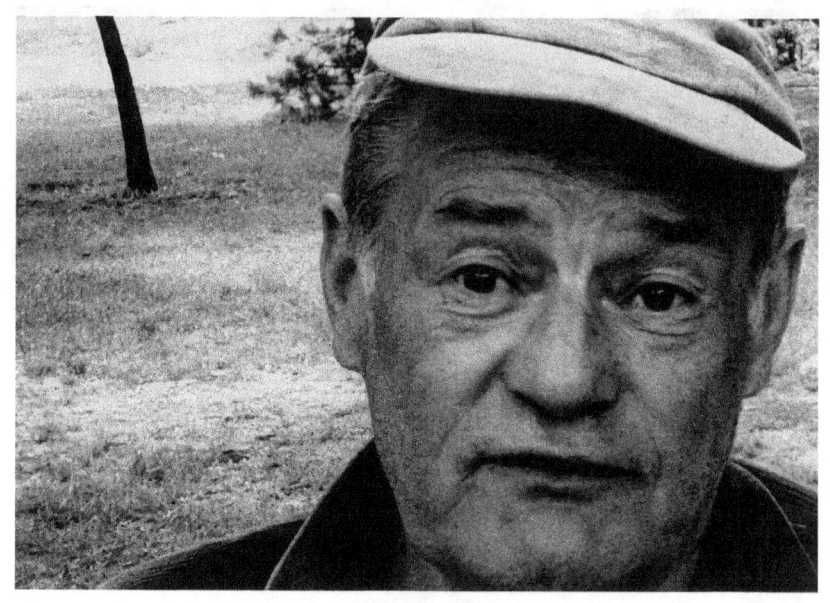

Talk to me

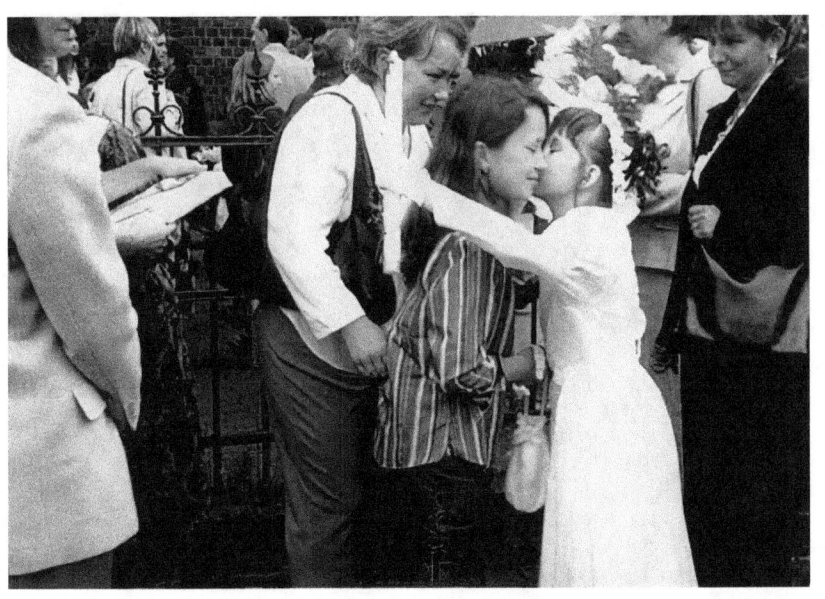

Church – first communion

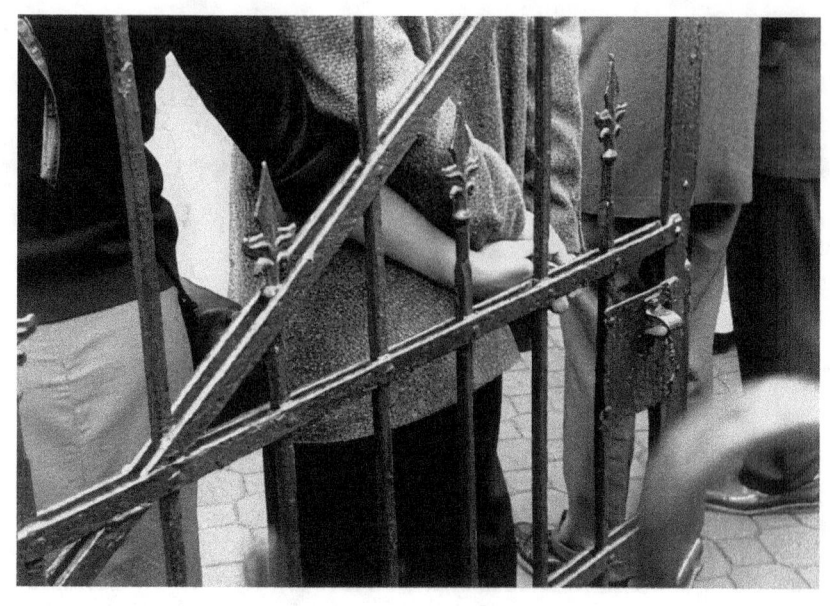

Church – first communion

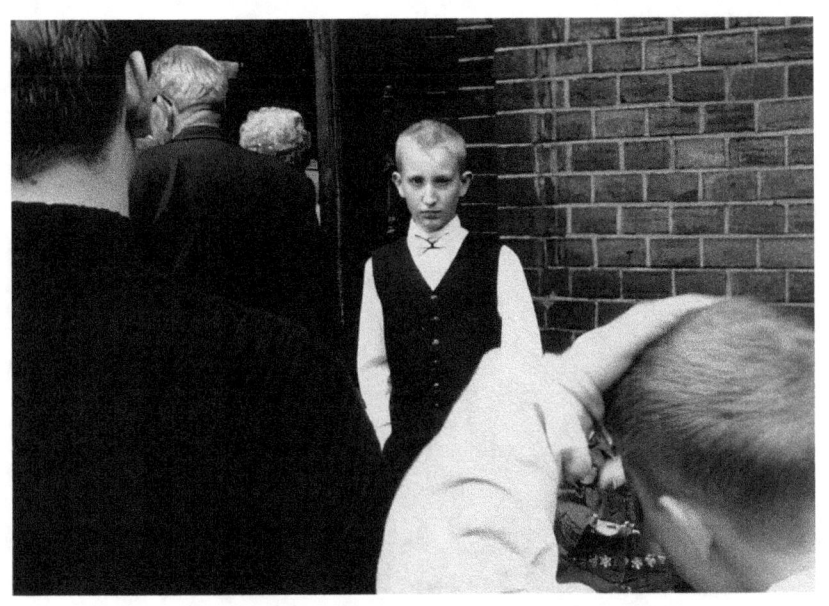

Church – first communion

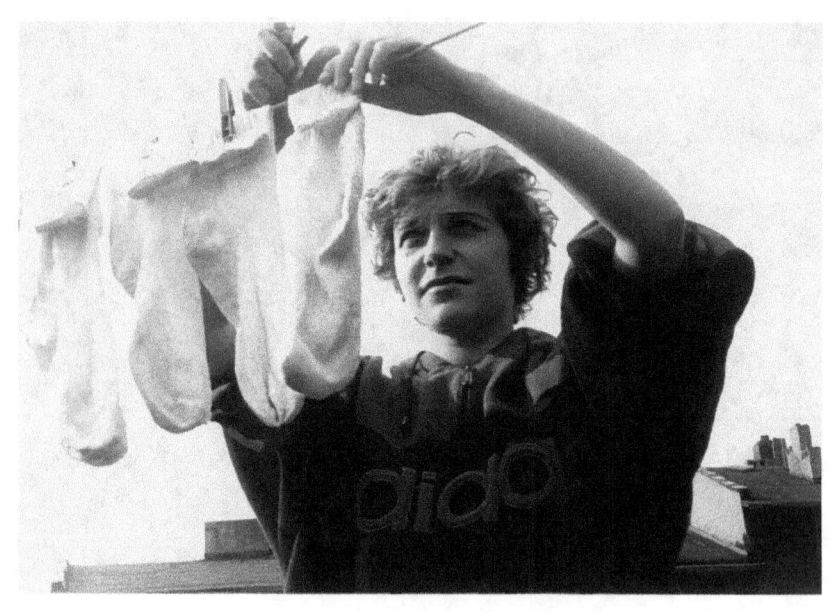

Ordinary activity

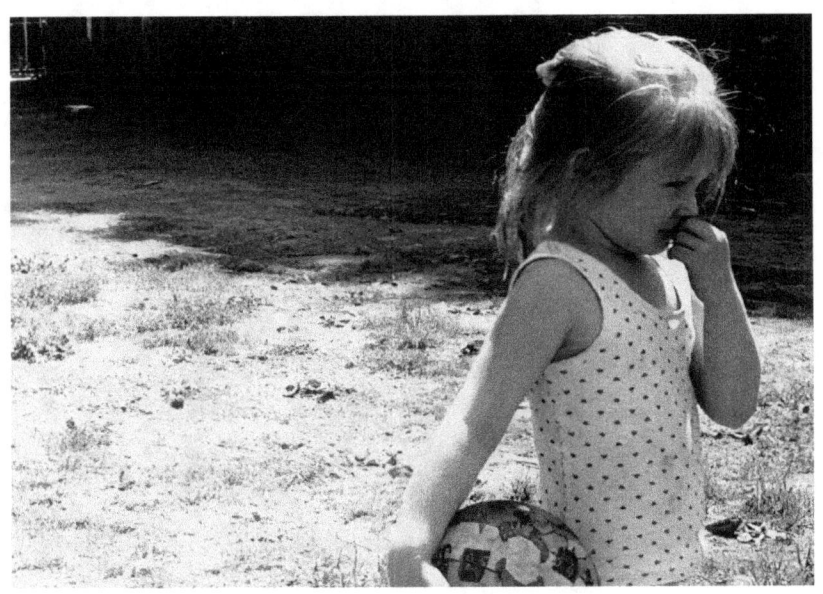

The game

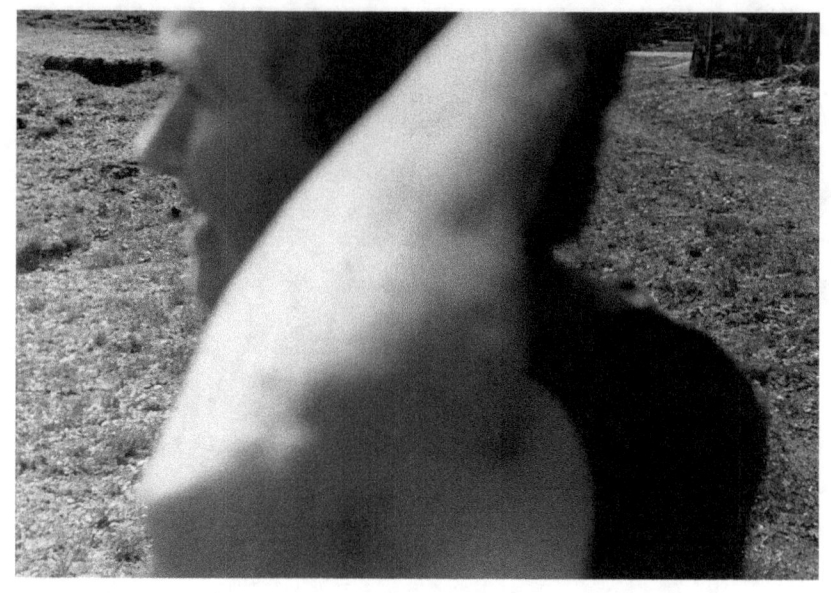

Eve's elbow

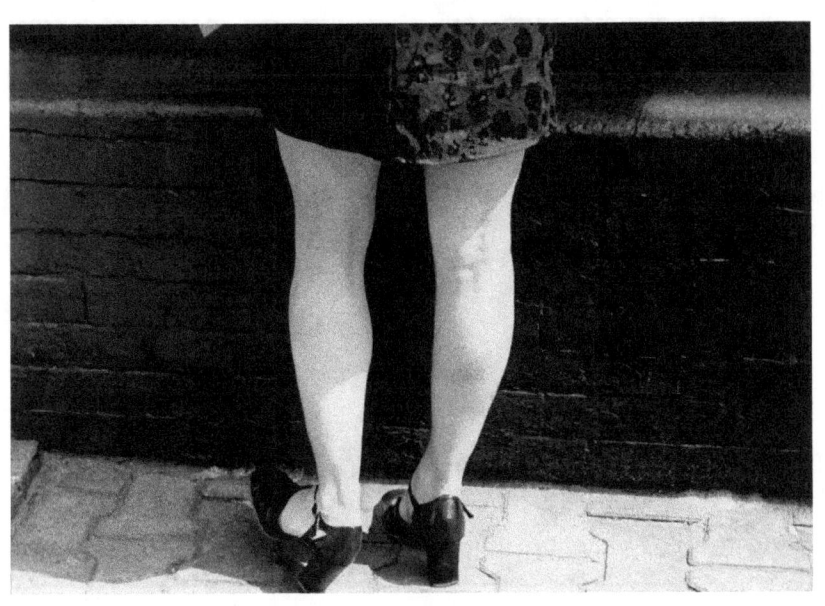

Parallelism

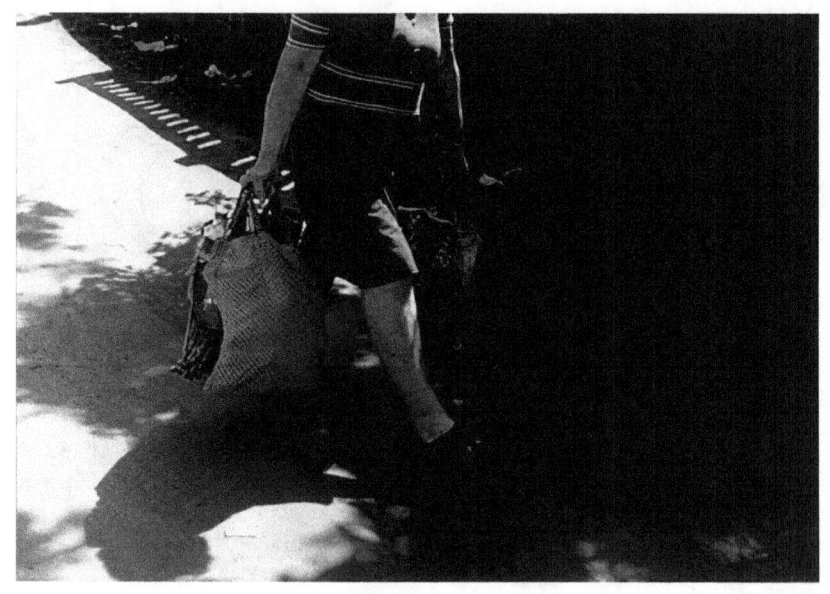

Weightlifting

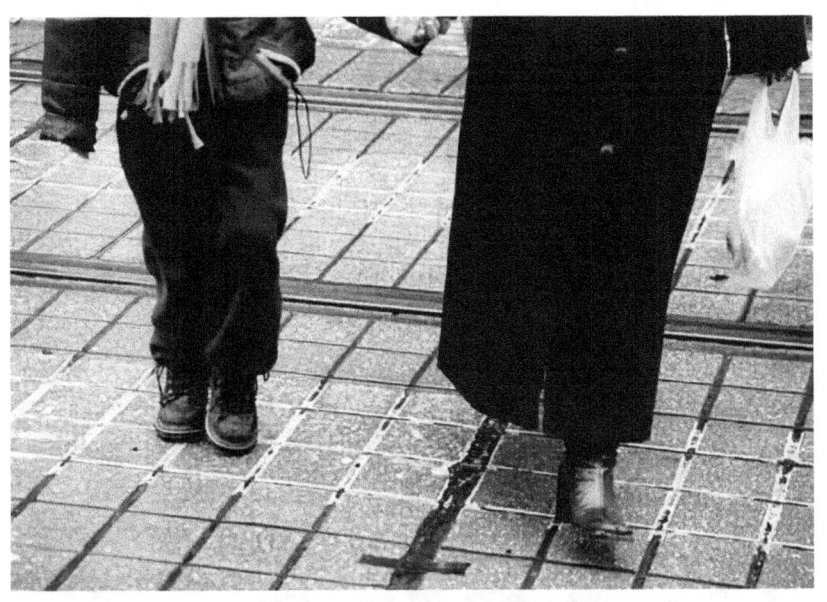

Holding the hand

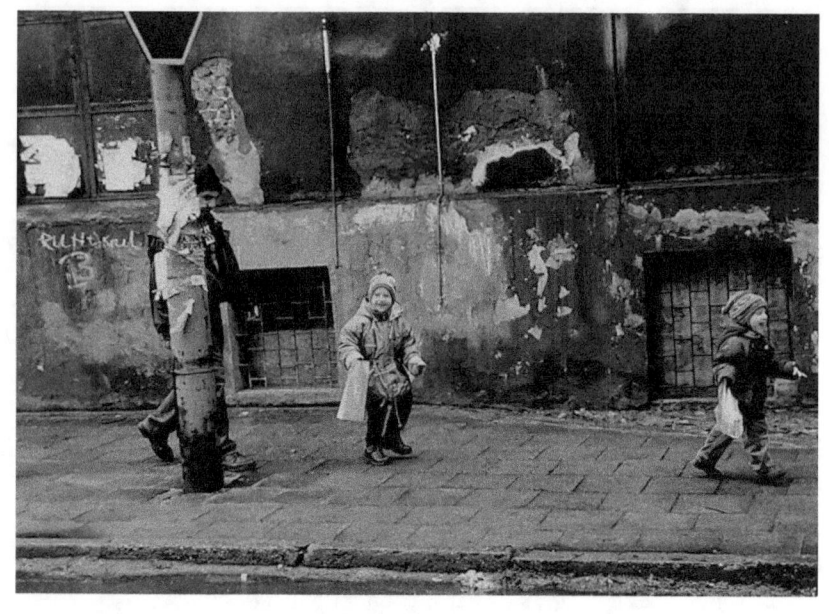

Lords of the city

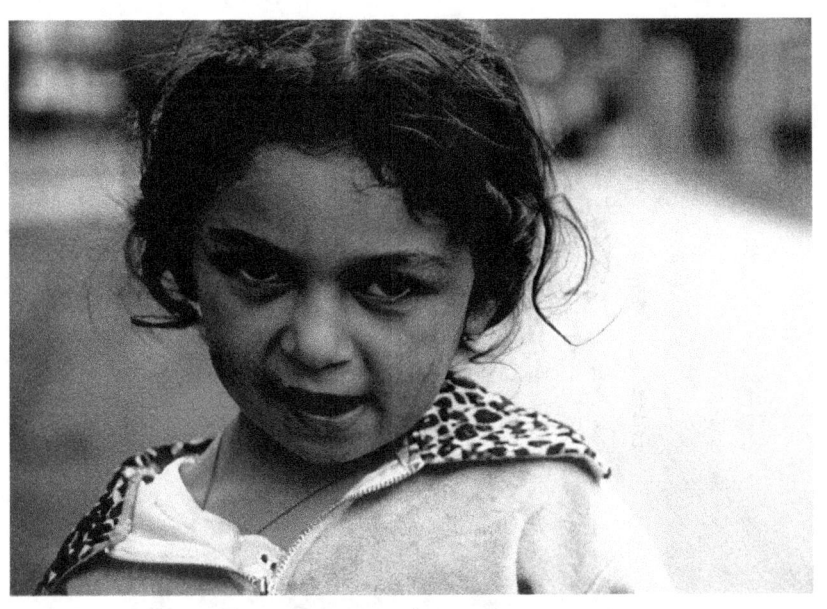

A Little Princess

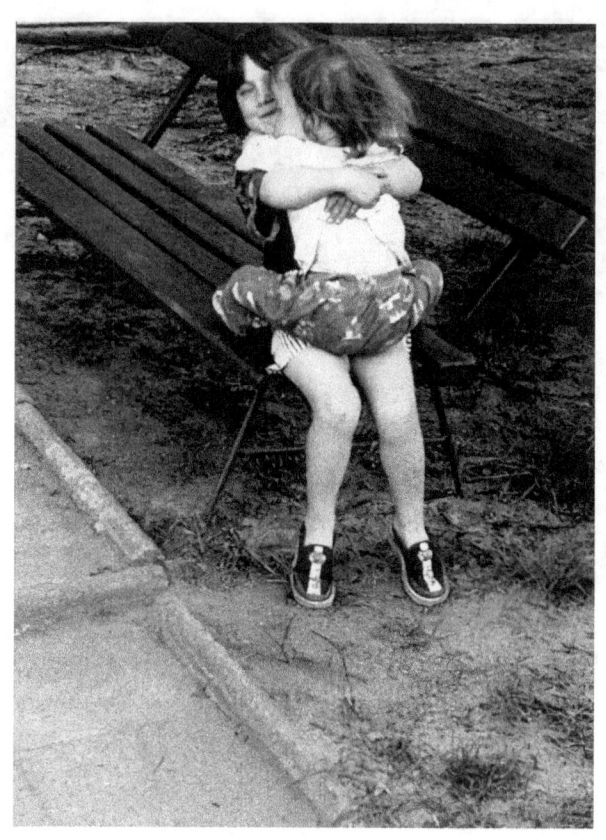

Friends.

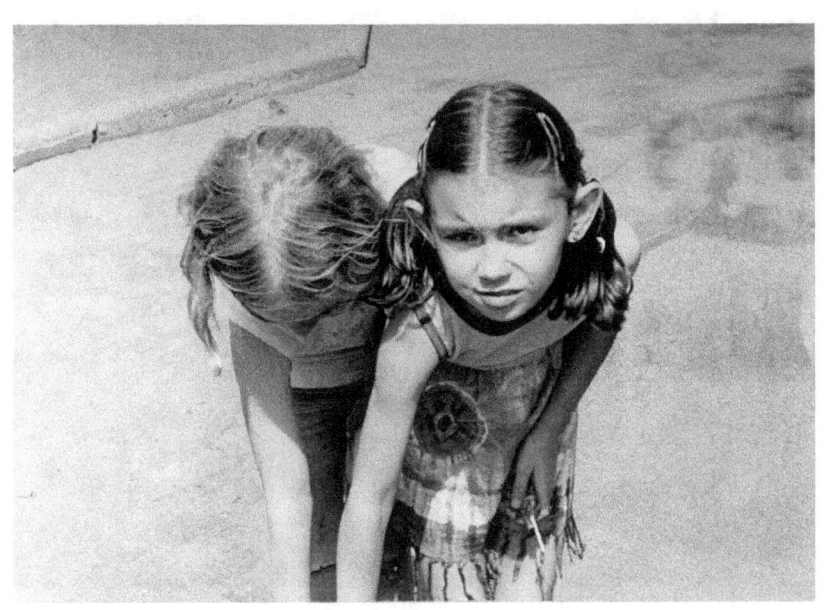

Friends

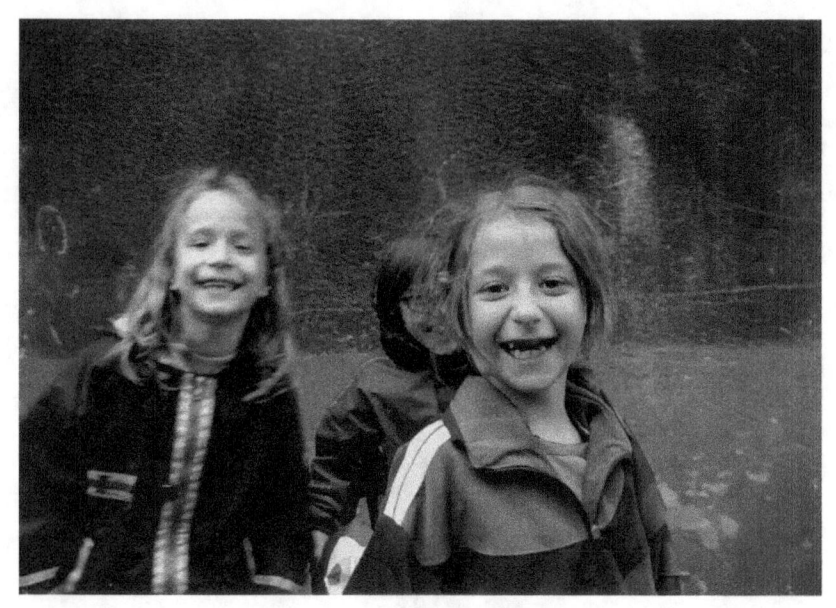

Friends

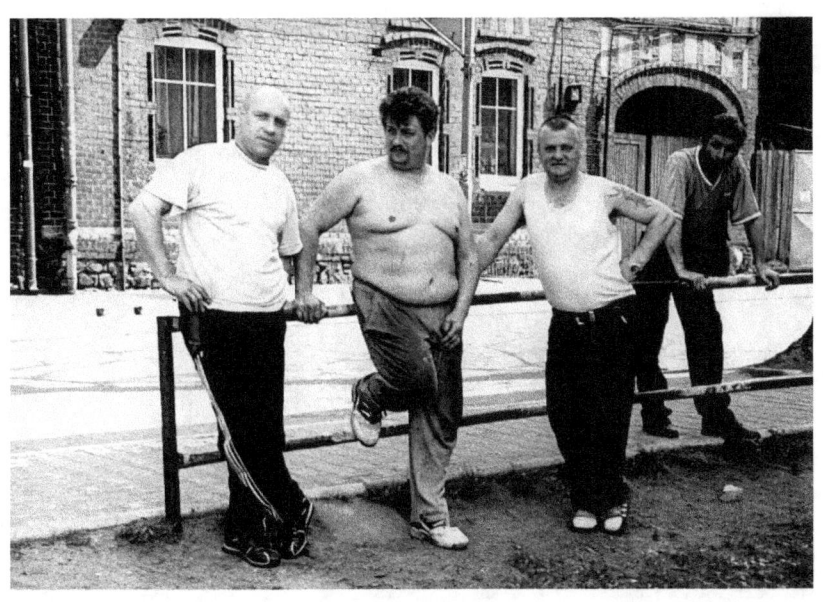

Colleagues

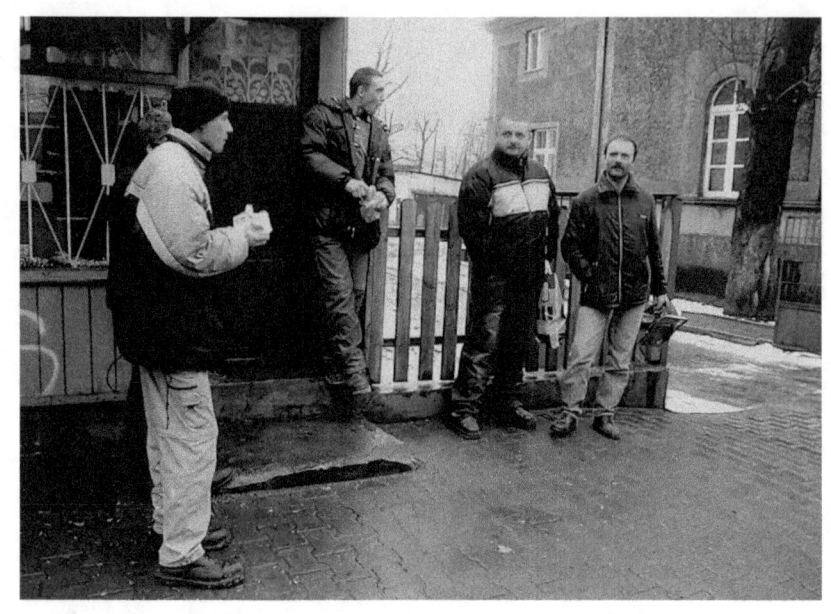

Acquaintances

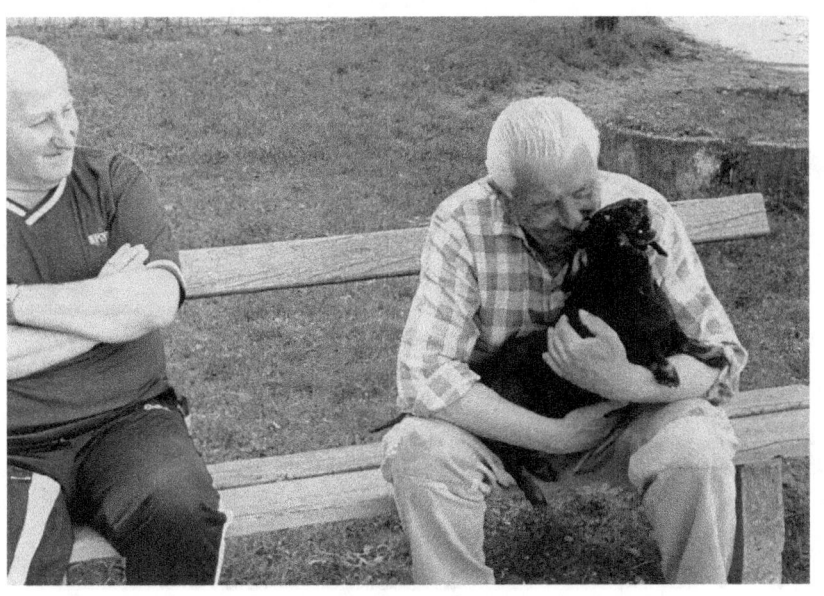

A man loves a dog, the dog loves man

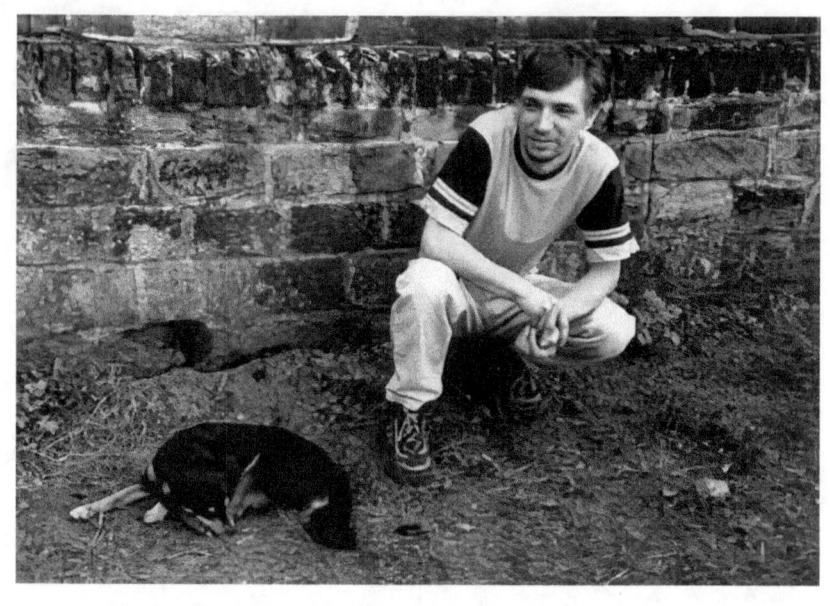

A man loves a dog, the dog loves man

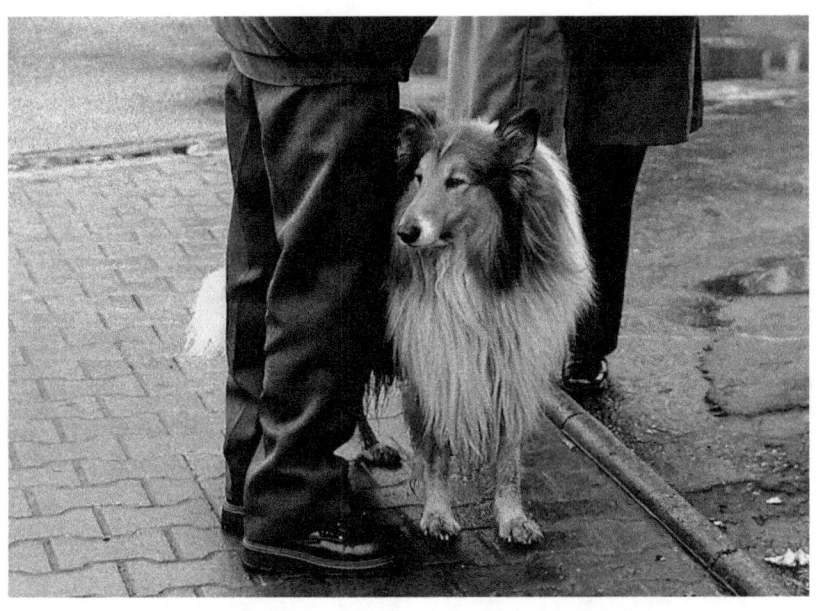

A man loves a dog, the dog loves man

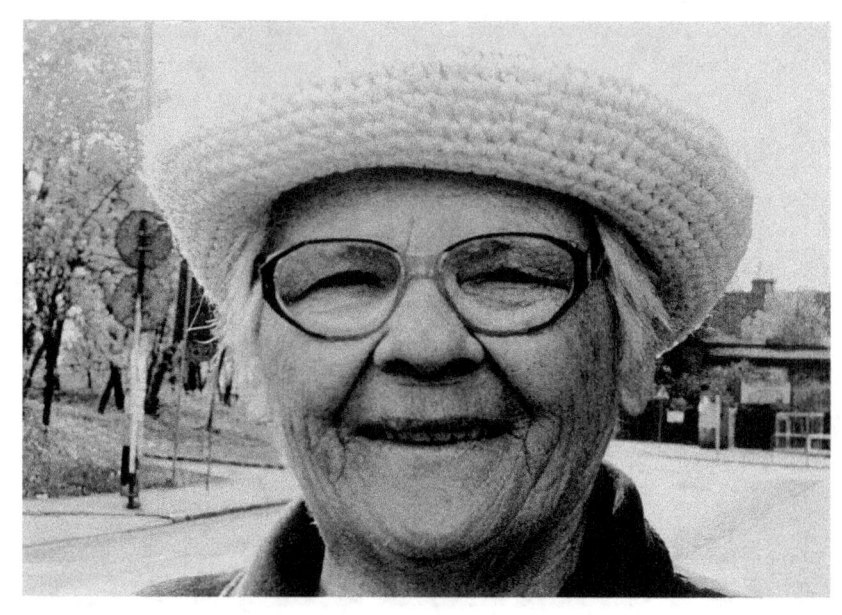

Can you take a photo?

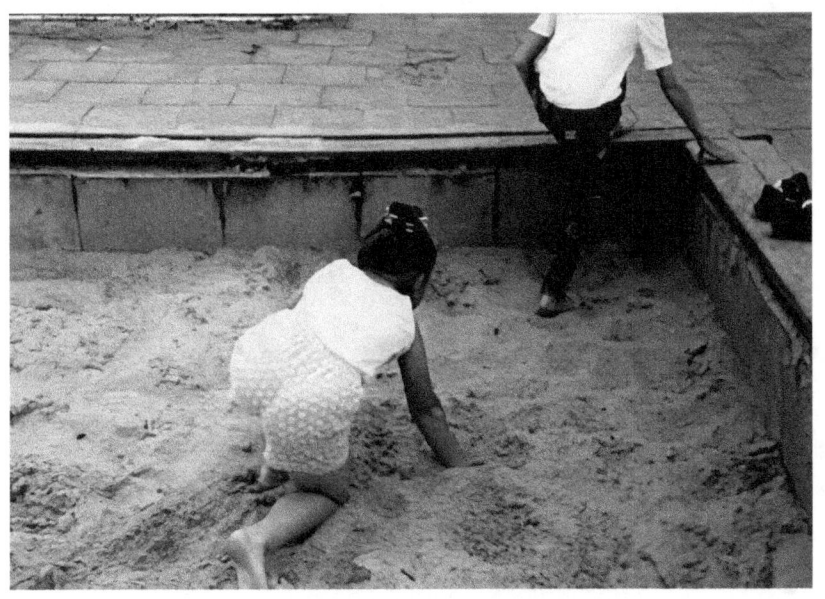

Output from the square

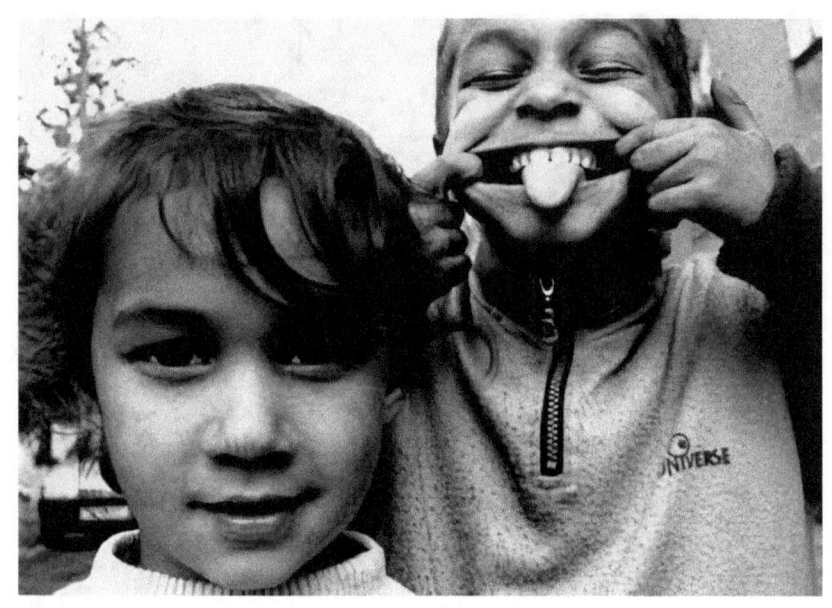

Keep smile

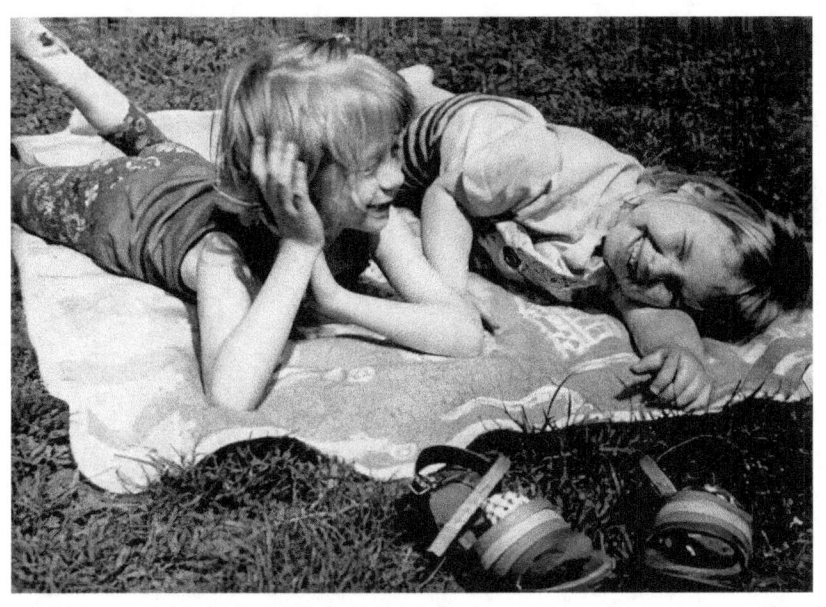

On the green grass

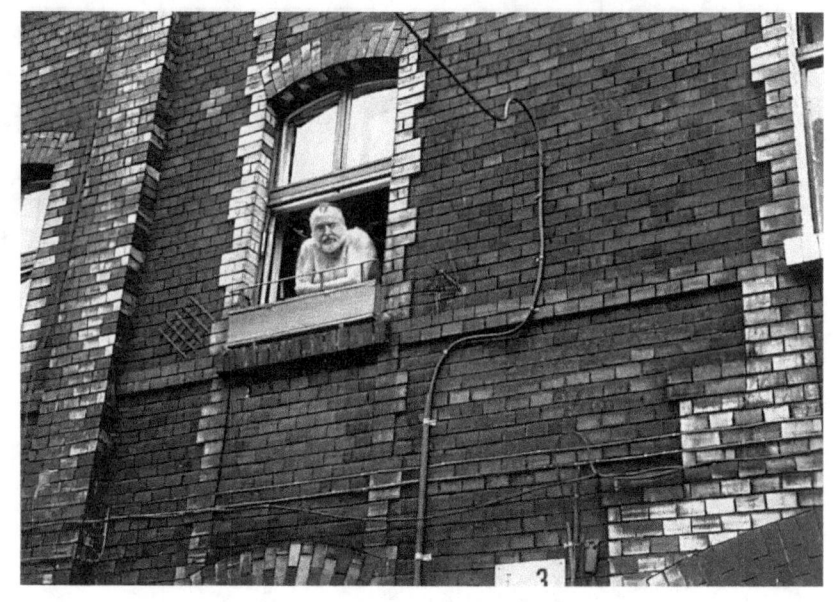

Looking at the world

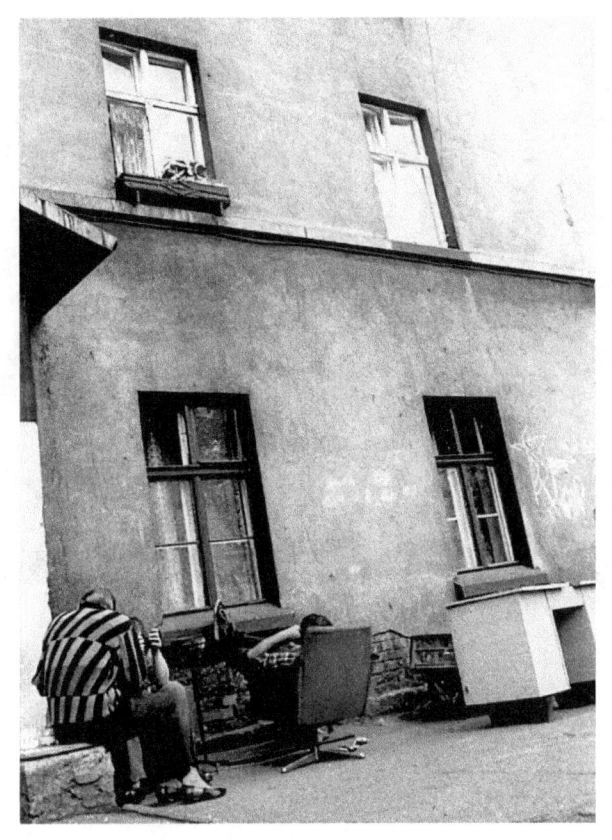

Afternoon

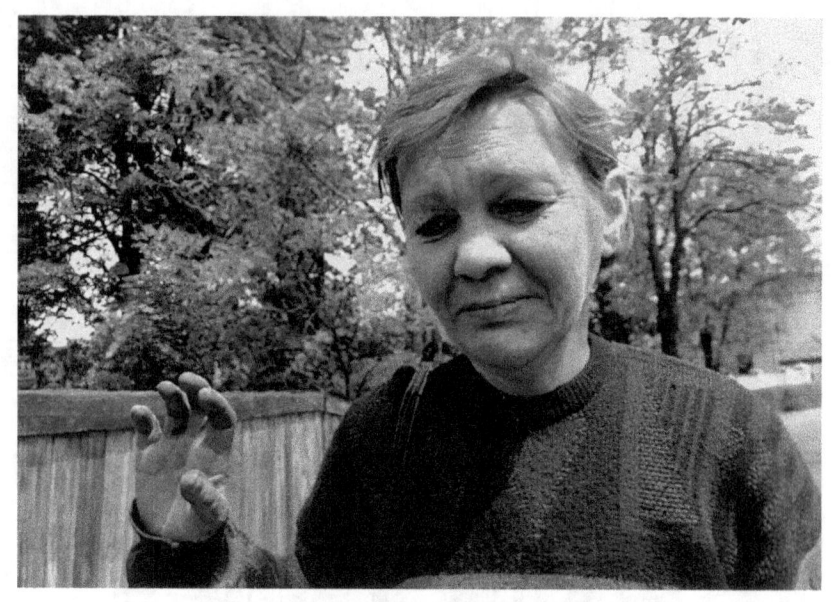

As soon as I recall

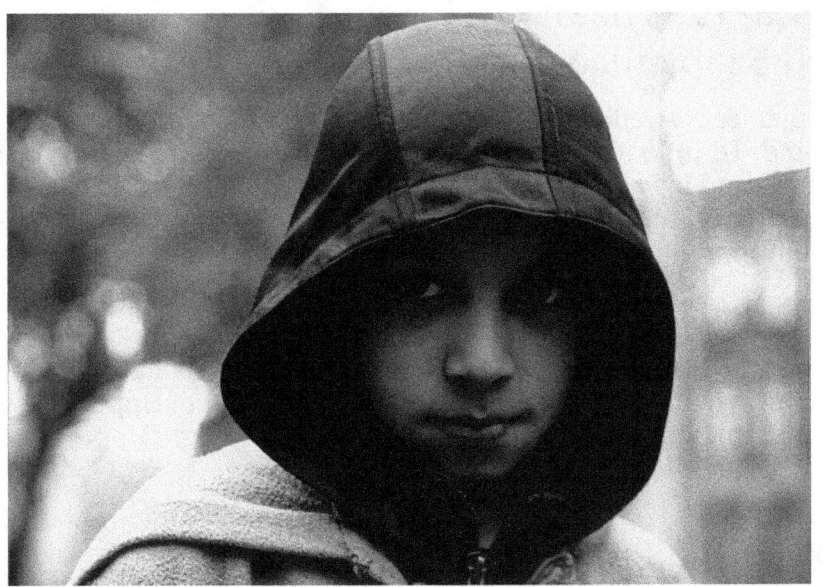
Looking through the eyes

About the History of Upper Silesia and Szopienice

Szopienice is a Katowice district, the city on the upper Silesia, in Poland. To 1960 it was independent. Szopienice founded as a village in 1360 and it was developed in the second half of the nineteenth century around the metallurgy industry. The civic rightist was given to it in 1951.

Upper Silesia to the thirteenth century, was part of the Polish. From the XIV it was in the Czech Crown. In 1742, it moved for the most part to the Prussia. Since 1870, together with Prussia have been it in the German Reich. In 1922, the south-eastern part of Upper Silesia with Szopienice was incorporated to the Polish. 1945 - Upper Silesia is in Polish and Czechoslovak borders.

About the Book

I photographed Szopienice in the spring of 2003. Suggested me to do an exhibition in the local community center. As its subject I chose the people from the streets of the district of Katowice. I was rather well received. No one was aggressive towards me, but not always my job was accepted. The first pictures I did in March 2003, finished in May. The exhibition took place in June.

About the Author

Jacek Lidwin has photographed for over 15 years. He regularly publishes, writes and talks about his work. His photos have featured in many publications and he has produced artwork and promotional images for artists, theatres and newspapers. He was exhibited in various exhibitions in Poland, mostly in Katowice where he works and lives.

Write to him: jaceklidwin@gmail.com

www.ingramcontent.com/pod-product-compliance
Lightning Source LLC
Chambersburg PA
CBHW050316220526
45465CB00005B/2012